Helping Abused Children

*A book for those who work
with sexually abused children*

By Patricia Kehoe, Ph.D.

Published by
Parenting Press, Inc.
P.O. Box 15163
Seattle, WA   98115

ISBN 0-943990-18-1 paper
ISBN 0-943990-41-6 library binding
LC 86-62635

TABLE OF CONTENTS

INTRODUCTION

Some facts about sexual abuse:

Research tells us that up to 38% of all girls experience at least some form of sexual contact with an adult prior to their 18th birthday.

As many as one out of every ten boys (10%) experience sexual abuse before that same age.

Only a small fraction (1/5) of all sexual abuse cases are ever reported to agencies. This is especially true if the victim is a boy.

Roughly a third of victims are molested by a parent, another third are abused by a parent-substitute, and the remaining third are victimized by a non-family member, often known to the child, such as a babysitter or teacher. As many as 75 to 85% of abusers are previously known by their victims in some capacity.

As many as 50% of adult women who experienced sexual abuse during childhood continue to report at least some on-going difficulties related to the experience. The remaining 50% report no ongoing problems due to childhood sexual abuse (Finkelhor, 1984, 1986).

Both sexually and physically abused children are found in disproportionate numbers among troubled teenaged populations, such as drug abusers, runaways and juvenile offenders. While clearly not every victimized child becomes so severely disturbed, it does appear that victimization may increase a child's risk of these problems.

Child sexual abuse can be defined as the sexual use of a child or adolescent by an adult for his or her own sexual gratification, without regard for the child's consent, development or emotional attachment, through manipulation, threats, or physical force.

During the past two decades, public recognition of the problems of physical and sexual abuse of children has increased rapidly. While some interpret this as an indicator of a new epidemic of maltreatment, the evidence available to us strongly suggests that all forms of child abuse have long been present in society, but were simply unrecognized.

Even mental health professionals who were often confronted with direct evidence of all forms of child abuse tended to underestimate its frequency and to ascribe it to only the most disturbed segments of our population. My graduate training in clinical psychology in the early '70s did not specifically address the problems of physically or sexually victimized children.

Colleagues in other mental health professions verify that there was a similar gap in theoretical and practical information on the subject in their training. As I gained experience as a practicing psychologist, I was astounded by the extent of this problem. The more often I ventured to ask questions about child abuse, the more often it would seem to materialize.

The beginnings of *Something Happened and I'm Scared to Tell* were generated by the need for materials to aid the process of therapeutic intervention with the very young victim of sexual abuse. My own sense of helplessness in dealing with a two or three year old victim who lacked even the vocabulary to describe his experiences pointed toward a need for support materials.

Unlike most victims of physical abuse, sexually abused children do not always show visible scars or bruises. Their words and behaviors are often the only way we can recognize the emotional scars and prevent additional damage. The cognitive and emotional developmental level of the preschooler may also increase the potential damage done by child abuse since the child lacks the ability to rationalize or identify with other victims.

When I observed first-hand the positive effects of children's books dealing with feelings about various life events such as divorce, or the birth of a sibling, I began to picture a children's book which would incorporate simple information, vocabulary and emotional reassurance geared to the youngest victim.

The book attempts to deal with some of the very individual kinds of fears and fantasies that are most common with young victims. It is intended as a starting point and aid to therapeutic intervention, not as a substitute for professional evaluation and treatment. Sensitive, individualized treatment, as well as the level of cooperation between parents and the various social service, legal, and mental health professionals involved, are the most critical determinants of how a child will eventually handle the experience of sexual abuse.

Something Happened and I'm Scared to Tell is aimed at all of the groups who deal with the suspected or identified pre-school to seven year old victim of sexual abuse. Parents, educators, social service workers, court personnel, and therapists will find the book helpful as part of their coordinated efforts to work with young victims.

This accompanying handbook attempts to provide some basic background information on sexual abuse, child development, and the ways in which young children respond to sexual abuse and its aftermath. Suggested activities, games, and books relevant to prevention and identification are included for parents and educators. A brief overview of some useful therapeutic activities is included. These suggestions form only a part of the therapeutic process, and are not a substitute for therapy itself. A guided reading of *Something Happened...* is included to highlight some of the major concepts in the book and to suggest possible interactions. Finally, a summary of key books in the areas of child development, parenting, and child abuse is presented. Those listed are personal favorites, and represent information that has been particularly helpful to me, rather than exhaustive surveys of their areas.

PREVENTION

No discussion of such a potentially traumatic
experience as sexual abuse can be complete without
first emphasizing prevention. Once one becomes aware
of the truly large scale of sexual victimization of our
children, the need for effective preventive strategies on
the part of society, educators, and parents is readily
apparent. When we also recall that a small, but
significant, minority of victimized children go on to
victimize others in a continuing cycle of maltreatment,
prevention becomes even more urgent.

In recent years, there has been a massive increase in
educational materials on child abuse prevention,
particularly those aimed directly at children. The
widespread use of videotapes has brought new material
directly into the home at the parents' discretion; but
parents rightly express anxiety about the competing
needs of helping children become a trusting adults
while still protecting them from danger.

The best of the books and videotapes make use of
some important information about the identity of sex
offenders. This knowledge includes the fact that the
majority of victims know their abusers, and that the
majority of these cases occur within a family setting.
With this in mind, the stereotype of the "dirty old
man" lurking by the playground becomes much less
typical.

Indeed, materials which focus almost exclusively on
sexual abuse outside the family may be doing
concerned parents a disservice by lulling them into the
false belief that their children are somehow protected
from sexual abuse. Many of the current books and
films can help us teach children how to protect
themselves from the dangerous situation of abduction.
However, the risk of sexual victimization by a known
and trusted adult is far greater.

Educating children to recognize, avoid, and report sexual abuse by a trusted adult is clearly a far more complex task than simply teaching them who is a stranger and who is not. One element of prevention requires all those who care for children, from future parents and teachers to babysitters and health care providers, to disregard stereotypes about child abuse and learn how to recognize and respond to high risk situations. Parents, schools, churches, and organized youth groups can all be part of this continuing educational process.

The second area of prevention must focus on the social factors which contribute to tolerance of child abuse. A view of children as private property of their parents, the exploitation of child sexuality for advertising purposes, and the prevalence of violence in the media are but a few of the relevant social issues to be considered.

A third preventive strategy is the overall improvement of parenting skills and knowledge of child development in our society. Any training or experience which prepares caregivers to build children's self esteem, encourage open discussion of problems, and address sexual issues without fear, will indirectly help to prevent child abuse. Parenting classes, support groups, and child development classes in secondary schools are just some of the ways to bring this information to current and future parents.

In the rest of this section, more aspects of prevention will be discussed: building self-esteem, improving trust and communication, and sex education. Ideas for building children's skills in these areas will be presented, along with activities and references to assist parents and educators.

BUILDING SELF ESTEEM

While we cannot prevent abusers from approaching our children or, in many instances, from actually initiating sexual abuse, we *can* make our children more difficult targets for intimidation. Children who feel good about themselves, who receive physical affection when needed, and who know that they are valued by their parents, are more likely to trust their own instincts in a stressful situation. Most importantly, they are also likely to feel safe in telling someone about it. They are less apt to be manipulated by the "special" or threatening aspects of the ongoing, abusive relationship.

SUGGESTIONS
Some general guidelines for enhancing self esteem in children will be included here as examples.

• Realistic, age-appropriate standards for behavior and performance.

• Emphasis on the positive, through loving touches, compliments, and praise for good behavior.

• Constructive criticism when positive reinforcement alone is not sufficient. This is the ability to correct unacceptable behavior without the use of name calling or other humiliating tactics.

• Good child, bad behavior. Focus anger on the unacceptable behavior and not on the total person.

ACTIVITIES
Many everyday activities provide opportunities for reinforcing self-esteem. One straightforward favorite which I often use in therapy is *"I like you because...I like me because...."* When children see trusted adults feel comfortable complimenting themselves, they are much more likely to be able to give and accept compliments themselves. Children who reject compliments given by others often give valuable clues about the areas in which they feel inadequate and why.

REFERENCES

One of the older titles is still my favorite in this area: *Your Child's Self Esteem* by Dorothy Corkille-Briggs.

A thought-provoking book on unrealistic modern expectations of children is *The Hurried Child* by David Elkind. It gives many examples of adults' unwitting pushes into maturity for which children are often unprepared.

For parents who want more information on just what they can expect developmentally from their child, the Gesell Institute's series on *Your Two Year Old*, *Your Three Year Old*, etc., remains a good choice.

TRUST AND COMMUNICATION SKILLS

When we discuss development of trust and communication skills in young children, we must include the basic ability to recognize what we think of as a "feeling" in the first place. Next is the ability to communicate that feeling verbally.

As youngsters go from communicating their internal states primarily by crying, as in infancy, to gradually substituting verbal statements for tears and tantrums, we think of them as "growing up." This is precisely what their developing verbal skills allow them to do.

The skills involved in recognizing and expressing a feeling are important in preventing childhood exploitation because they train a child to trust his own feelings and to know that parents will listen. The following suggestions can help the child learn the process of identifying, labelling and expressing feelings.

SUGGESTIONS

Modelling: The old axiom "Do as I say, not as I do" is a good example of what will *not* work in teaching children how to express their emotions. Children will imitate the behavior of loved and respected adults in their environment with amazing expertise. How they see us express our anger, sadness, and love will have far more impact on their behavior than any instructions we try to give.

Feelings vs. Behavior: The process of distinguishing between feelings and behavior goes on throughout our lifetime. Who has not experienced stabs of guilt just for *feeling* dislike or anger toward someone we are supposed to love completely? For children, this differentiation between *how* they express their feelings vs. *what* they feel, is itself part of the larger effort to distinguish fantasy from reality. Statements such as "It's okay to be angry, but it's not okay to hit" can help a child to distinguish feelings from behavior.

Even general reassurance that it is okay to be sad, lonely, mad, etc., lets the child know that feelings themselves are not harmful. Rigid expectations that all expressions of feelings should be calm, rational, or brief, are also confusing to children.

Active listening: This is listening on two channels at once in order to hear both *what* is being said and *how* it is being said.

Adults can then show some understanding of the child's experience by reflecting the child's feeling, clarifying it, or simply empathizing. For example, an angry child stalks to the dinner table after being called away from a favorite TV show. A parent can ignore this completely, criticize the moody behavior, or acknowledge that it can be frustrating to be interrupted. The last choice lets the child know his feelings do count.

Active listening is a way in which adults clearly demonstrate to children that feelings are never "right" or "wrong," but that feelings simply "are."

Physical punishment: Almost everyone who works with children is in favor of discipline that teaches self control, but there is much less agreement on what constitutes effective discipline.

In the present context, it is important to emphasize that regular use of physical punishment by parents or schools teaches children the importance of fear in controlling their behavior. More extreme uses of physical punishment teach them that children may be hurt by adults who love them. While no one could reasonably claim that physical punishment makes children more likely to be sexually abused, it can make children more fearful of reporting sexual abuse.

Frequent use of physical punishment, particularly when it is institutionalized as in some school systems, also makes it difficult for a child to believe that he is loved and respected as a person even when his behavior is not acceptable. Other disciplinary techniques, such as "Time Out" or loss of privileges, etc., can be even more effective than physical punishment. Many excellent books on disciplinary techniques are available to help adults choose non-violent, age-appropriate responses to undesirable behaviors. A few of these will be mentioned below.

ACTIVITIES

Drawing: Younger children will enjoy drawing to express feelings. Even non-representational art can represent "feeling sad." Finger painting allows very active artistic effort and is multi-sensory, providing the opportunity for labelling feelings in a fun situation.

Games: School age children will enjoy a game called "The Talking, Feeling and Doing Game" (Creative Therapeutics). This game focuses on questions and interactions and will illustrate the distinction between thinking, feeling and doing; the game reinforces the concept that feelings are okay even if some behavior is not.

Books and Media: Children of all ages can identify with feelings of characters in pictures, books, and TV shows without much difficulty. This can encourage family discussion and offers opportunities to bring up personal reactions.

REFERENCES
One of my favorite books on listening to children is by Mr. Rogers. His book, *Mr. Rogers Talks to Parents* gives some developmental

information on typical concerns many children have, while illustrating the many forms children's communication about sensitive topics can take.

Quick as a Cricket by Audrey Wood is a colorful children's book that uses lively illustrations to list the many contradictory feelings that make up each unique person. It is an excellent jumping off point for many games and activities about feelings.

The Runaway Bunny, a children's classic by Margaret Wise Brown, tells a story about the persistence of parental love, which even misbehavior cannot change. It is wonderfully reassuring for children to know that parents will love them no matter how hard they try to run away.

Where the Wild Things Are by Maurice Sendak: allows both parents and children to enjoy this exciting tale of a boy whose angry feelings start to get out of control and cause him some trouble. The acceptance of occasional misbehavior, the use of firm, calm discipline, and Max's use of fantasy to gain a sense of control and self-esteem again, give children a clear example of all kinds of ways to handle angry feelings.

The Magic Years by Selma Freiberg, is a classic book which gives us a glimpse into the private, emotional world of the young child.

Everyone Makes Mistakes is a videotape of one of the segments on a Golden Book video of Sesame Street characters. It is a simple story of learning to tolerate yourself when you are less than perfect and is a real self-esteem builder for children.

How to Discipline with Love by Fitzhugh Dodson, contains a comprehensive discussion of loving discipline for children of all ages.

Parent Effectiveness Training by Thomas Gordon, has become one of the best known approaches to parenting and it deserves its reputation. PET is especially strong in the area of listening skills and conflict resolution.

SEX EDUCATION
The following suggestions for educating the toddler and preschooler about sexuality focus on ways to help a child feel good about his or her body and about talking with adults about sexual issues without fear.

SUGGESTIONS

Teach children to be on a first name basis with their bodies. The longer I work with sexually abused children, the less tolerant I become toward "cute"

11

names for the sex organs. Aside from the message that genitals cannot be politely discussed without using a pseudonym, there is difficulty in convincing bureaucracies such as court systems that "my lucy" really does refer to a child's vagina. It can mean the difference in whether a child's testimony is fully believed or discounted.

Sex education vs. the facts of life. The facts of life...the phrase implies a sheet of information that is given to a child on a one time basis. Sex education is a far more time consuming process that continues in developmentally graded steps. It allows us to teach positive feelings about sexuality by establishing that sexual feelings are okay even if a particular sexual behavior is not acceptable in all circumstances.

Initiate sexual discussion. Adults can bring up sexual topics first. Parents and schools can make books about sex available and parents can read them together with the child.

The choice of anatomically correct toys gives another powerful message about open sexual communication. I often wonder how children would feel about the head and its meaning in our society if all dolls and animals came without a head in its accustomed place. The lack of genitals can present a powerful non-verbal message about what more than one child has described to me as "the nasty parts."

Whose body is it? Adults can show respect for children's feelings about when and how, and even if, they wish to be physically touched. To allow a child to make choices about giving and receiving affection communicates that he is respected. Most importantly, it demonstrates his right to limit who, when, and how he is touched. Affectionate relatives may have difficulty with this, but will generally understand if parents tactfully explain. (See "The Family Code," below.)

ACTIVITIES

The Naming Game. Even very young toddlers love to practice naming things. We can use this opportunity to include in a matter-of-fact way the genitals as we teach children about their bodies, or through the use of a toy or doll.

Role Playing. Role plays have the advantage of adapting to almost every age and ability level. Young children will need more adult assistance to structure the beginning of a role play, while older children can often generate their own situations around a particular topic.

Parents can use *It's My Body* and *No More Secrets For Me* as starting points for role plays which gradually include practicing how to handle situations ranging from the unwanted hug of a visiting relative to a direct attempt of sexual abuse. "The Family Code," one of several suggested preventive activities included in *Protect Your Child*, allows any family member to use a code word to indicate an uncomfortable touch. Parents agree to honor and support that child's code by politely but firmly explaining family rules to overly-affectionate adults.

REFERENCES

Two excellent books on sexuality are *Where Do Babies Come From?* (Sheffred), suitable for the younger child, and the more detailed *Where Did I Come From?* (Mayle), which is humorously illustrated and will be of interest to school age children. These books provide information and limitless possibilities for parent-child discussion.

It's My Body (Freeman) is an excellent, straightforward book that empowers children to say "NO" to an adult. The author offers them information to use which allows them to plan and practice a response in advance—a key method of handling a crisis at any age.

No More Secrets For Me (Wachter) lets children from approximately kindergarten age and up consider vignettes about the various forms of sexual abuse and how they can be handled. While the very young child is unlikely to be able to connect the situations, the older child will learn that different people can victimize children in different ways.

IDENTIFICATION

Identifying the warning signals of abuse is a particularly difficult task with young children because of their limited knowledge and experience. Since even the best efforts at prevention will not guarantee that a child cannot be manipulated, especially by a trusted or loved adult, early identification is especially important in the prevention of ongoing sexual abuse. Because children think and behave differently at different ages, some of the clues they may use to communicate their underlying concerns are also different as they develop.

The following section includes some of the more common manifestations of sexual abuse at different ages. The list is neither complete nor in itself conclusive, but all of the following signs suggest the need for careful evaluation of the child and circumstances involved.

WARNING SIGNS

Toddler and Pre-School Children

A. *Unusual physical symptoms.* Even infants can be sexually victimized, although fortunately, this seems to be comparatively rare. The only clues in such instances tend to be physical ones that may be uncovered during a regular check-up. It is a good precautionary measure to have a pediatrician check out any persistent, unexplained vaginal or rectal discharge and rashes.

B. *Change in daily behavior routines.* As children become more aware of their environment, they begin to react to many kinds of stress, often with a change in eating, sleeping, or behavior patterns.

The difficulty for parents who suspect possible abuse is that many changes, such as increases in nightmares or preoccupation with monsters between ages two and three, are often part of normal development. Parents have to be sensitive to any hints that increased fearfulness, separation anxiety, or "clinginess" are more than normal transitory, adjustment patterns. Often, children's responses to an abusive situation are more intense or more long lasting than would be expected under ordinary circumstances. Again, parental familiarity with developmental norms is essential.

C. *Sexual preoccupation*. A sudden increase in masturbation is normally noted during the time of toilet training and again around age three. In comparison, sexually abused children often display a more intense preoccupation with masturbation, ignoring other play activities, or making very definite attempts at direct sex play with other children.

Familiarity with specific sexual acts is another indication that the child has somehow been exposed to explicit sex. While this sometimes occurs through exposure to X-rated movies, it is in itself harmful and should be clearly checked out rather than assumed as the basis for the child's sudden knowledge.

D. *Increased aggressiveness*. A sudden, dramatic increase in aggression toward adults or peers is another possible indicator of either physical or sexual abuse.

E. *Avoidant behavior*. Children who show sudden fearfulness or avoidance of a previously liked individual should also be taken seriously. Adults can be faced with the difficult task of supporting the needs of a frightened child without jumping to conclusions or encouraging avoidant behavior in general.

F. *Play themes*. One other clue about sexual abuse can come from children while they play. In addition to the increase in sexual play with other children mentioned previously, fantasy play can tell us about a child's concerns. A teddy bear with a "secret" may need to talk to a grownup about a special problem.

G. *Normal sexual curiosity*. On a final note, parents can be reassured that sexual exploration in the same age children of either sex is common and natural. It is seldom harmful in any way unless adults react very harshly or inconsistently. Distraction is usually a good response to such situations.

School Age Children

A. *School problems*. One of the most sensitive indicators of how well children in this age range are coping overall is their ability to function in the intellectually and emotionally demanding school environment.

School requires attention, concentration, motivation, self control, peer interaction, and respect for authority. Children experiencing any significant life stressor will often demonstrate sudden, unexplained changes in academic achievement or behavior.

B. *Precocious sexuality*. In girls this age, prematurely sexualized behavior and dress may be noted. Given our society's tendency to turn normal, ten year olds into sexpots for advertising purposes this behavior can be difficult for adults to deal with. The pseudo-"sexy" behavior may hide a learned pattern of receiving attention for sexualized behavior. Boys this age may demonstrate a preoccupation with sexual jokes and comments that goes well beyond normal curiosity.

C. *Sexual identity problems*. This can range from recurrent statements about wanting to be a different sex to teasing by peers about a behavior that does not conform to stereotypes. Obviously, these issues are not always indicative of a problem but adults should be sensitive to any recurrent difficulties for the child in being "male" or "female."

D. *Chronic physical complaints*. A child with frequent, medically unexplained, physical complaints may be handling anxiety through sickness. Chronic symptoms of stress such as headaches and stomach aches can occur for a variety of reasons, but for a small subgroup, they are associated with victimization.

E. *Sexual activity with younger children.* Sexual activity with a much younger child may indicate the modeling of a traumatic event and should *always* be taken very seriously.

RESPONSES TO IDENTIFICATION

The Parent: Parents who are confronted with the reality of sexual abuse often feel overwhelmed. When the sex offender is someone outside the close circle of friends and family, there is often rage as well as fear of losing control and hurting the offender. Because parents struggle to protect their children, these angry feelings are understandable and justifiable. However, it is important to parent *and* child that this anger be channelled into socially acceptable behavior, such as filing charges, participating in citizens groups on victimization, etc. These steps allow parents to feel that they can make a contribution from their own experience, as well as provide support for others who have experienced similar feelings of helplessness and rage.

The second greatest difficulty for parents whose children have been abused by strangers or more distant adults is knowing how to share their feelings with their children. Clinical experience recommends that parents try to avoid the extremes. Either intense emotional upset in front of young children or excessive calmness to the point of denial of what has happened, can be frightening and confusing to the child. Parents who share some of their feelings in a supportive way can let the child know that they disapprove of the abusive behavior and will protect the child.

In instances where parents have tried to project a totally calm exterior while inwardly seething, children have later commented to me that their parents "didn't care" when told of sexual abuse. Similarly, parents who exploded or became hysterical have extra difficulty later on in convincing their children that they are upset at the abuser, not the child.

When the sex offender is a parent, family member, or trusted friend, the situation which confronts the parent(s) is particularly difficult. Dual loyalties may present the non-abusing parent with an impossible choice. The desire to protect a child may seem to be in direct competition with the desire to save a marriage or keep the family unit economically afloat. In some cases, physical violence between parents makes the non-abusive partner afraid of physical harm if the incident is reported.

In all of these situations, the first response of the parent is often disbelief. Usually, this has more to do with the initial shock of discovery than actual disbelief of the child. However, children faced with initial disbelief may later find it difficult to continue to speak out, even if the parent soon begins to accept their accounts.

The need to believe and protect the child cannot be over-emphasized. Outside agencies can help in these situations by giving the parent a chance to digest the information in private before bringing the child into the room. This lets the parent handle his or her own initial feelings before facing the child.

Parents who are confronted with allegations of incest, that is, sexual abuse within the immediate family, clearly have special problems in handling the identification of sexual abuse. Again, it is critical to believe the child unless there is very specific proof to the contrary. Unfortunately, the early denials of the alleged offender alone generally do not supply meaningful proof that no abuse occurred. The tendency of offenders to deny the seriousness of their behavior even to themselves, coupled with fears of criminal prosecution and family rejection, often combine to make the offender hope that charges will simply disappear if he or she waits long enough.

The non-abusive parent must often make the choice to protect the child without really knowing what actually occurred. Feelings of anger and resentment toward both child and abuser can be very upsetting. This parent may be horrified by her own resentment and suspect the child of "causing" the abuse in some way. Such feelings generally come from early training about the evils of childhood sexuality in any form.

Both the alleged abuser and the non-abusive family member will need professional assistance as soon as possible if they are to behave in ways which minimize the destructive impact on the child and family. Professionals who work in this area agree that reporting the sexual abuse to local child protective service teams is critical to the protection of all family members, including the abuser. One parent is almost never able to single-handedly prevent repetition of the abuse by another family member without outside assistance. Many support groups, such as Parents United, are also available to help families through this traumatic time.

One of the most common questions from parents in this situation is whether or not children lie about sexual abuse. My experience strongly suggests that children should be believed, especially by their parent(s), unless their allegations are clearly disproven. It is important for parents to communicate at least the willingness to believe, even if they feel further information is necessary. When parents automatically appear to believe another person over the child, basic trust is often impaired.

There appear to be only a few limited circumstances where children do not tell the truth about sexual abuse. In bitter custody and visitation battles, young children may be coached, bribed, or so confused by one parent's charges against the other that false accusations or half-truths are made. This kind of coaching always has a motive and is in itself another form of child abuse.

In other rare circumstances, older children, usually with a history of severe emotional and behavioral problems, may fabricate charges in some desperate attempt to punish or escape. Again, there is almost always a specific motive. It is important to note that even in most cases where the victim has severe emotional, behavioral, and family problems, the reports of sexual abuse are very real and should be thoroughly investigated.

The Child: Since the circumstances which surround sexual abuse can vary dramatically from violent to non-violent, as well as in terms of pain, chronicity, relationship with the abuser, and types of threats, there is no *one* way in which children can be said to experience sexual abuse. This section will present some of the more common themes and beliefs which sexually abused children share during the course of treatment.

View of the abuser: Adults are often surprised to find that children do not always dislike or even fear those who abuse them. Particularly if the abuser is a close friend or relative and the abuse is non-violent in nature, children may like aspects of the relationship and enjoy the affection they receive. Pleasurable sensations may cause the child guilt and confusion if only the "horrible" nature of the abuse is emphasized. In the case of an abusive parent, the child may actually fear the loss of the relationship if he or she reports the abuse. Children are often willing to tolerate even continued cruelty from parents and parent figures in return for any sign of love or kindness.

In other situations, children may fear telling about the abuse because they play the role of caretaker for the non-abusive parent. This type of role reversal can translate into a child who fears that the parent could not cope with the knowledge of abuse, or could not live without the abusive partner. Children who are old enough to recognize the "forbidden" sexual nature of the abuse may see the abuser as holding a powerful secret over their heads rather than recognizing that the reverse also holds true.

Common manipulations: The most common manipulation that adults use to ensure compliance from children is also the most obvious. The importance of love makes children vulnerable to many kinds of threats, especially when they have a close relationship with the abuser. Parents may threaten that their spouse "won't let me live here or see you anymore if you tell" or that the non-abusive spouse "will be very angry with me about what we've done." More destructive is the threat that someone close to the child will no longer love him or her if they learn of the abuse.

In more extreme cases, particularly involving someone who is close to the family but perhaps not as close to the child, the abuser may threaten directly to harm the child or someone whom the child loves, such as a parent, sibling, or grandparent. While these kinds of threats may seem unbelievable to an adult, the powerful position of adults in children's eyes may make even an absurd threat appear terrifyingly possible to the child victim.

Beliefs and fantasies: Children tend to respond to abusive experiences in some ways that seem illogical to adults. When we look at their reactions in light of their developmental levels, their responses make much more sense.

"Egocentric" thinking sounds like self-centered thinking to an adult. However, we also use this word to describe childish thinking because the child views himself as the center of his world. Egocentrism means that the child tends to view himself as responsible for everything that happens. Even very young children assign blame in the form of "badness" to themselves when problems with the family, such as divorce, occur. It is similar, if illogical, for children to conclude that they are in some way responsible for sexual abuse.

Older children, while less egocentric, are more able to generate reasons why they must be at fault in some way. This feeling of uniqueness also makes it very difficult for them to believe that anyone else could possibly have experienced something in the same or even a similar way. They are locked into an egocentric view of their experience by the fear that no one else could possibly understand. From these few examples, we can imagine why it can be so devastatingly difficult for children of any age to report sexual abuse.

Positive vs. negative outcomes: While each situation is unique, there do appear to be some general steps which can help to ensure the most positive outcome for a particular child. The first step, paradoxically the hardest for many parents, is reporting the abuse. This can bring a variety of support services, trained personnel and guidance for families dealing with a new and threatening situation.

Often offenders can assist in their victim's recovery at this point if they are willing to accept sole responsibility for their behavior. This can be the first step in freeing the child from a confusing web of guilt and a false sense of responsibility.

Willingness to protect the child from retribution or further abuse is also critical. Unfortunately, it is often the child who is removed from the home while abuse allegations are being investigated. This reinforces the child's belief that she is at fault or being punished. In addition, removal of the child increases the risk that the child may never return to the family and that the cycle of abuse will never really be confronted. Removal of the accused abuser during the investigative period is usually the best approach from the point of view of the child's interests.

Another critical factor in the child's ability to recover is the reassurance of continued love and support from at least one parent. The knowledge that he or she is not held responsible by the rest of the family for the sometimes devastating consequences of reporting abuse is critical to the victim. The damage of abuse is compounded if the non-abusive parent is rejecting or holds the child responsible for the behavior of the abuser. Families can work together and eventually stay together if they will acknowledge their problems and take joint steps to protect their children. Divorce or imprisonment are not the only possible outcomes of incest when there is cooperation between family, social service, and judicial personnel.

TREATMENT

WHY TREATMENT IS NECESSARY
A Developmental Perspective

Given the high incidence of sexual abuse among children, it is all too apparent that only a small percentage of victims will ever receive professional assistance in coping with the aftermath of abuse. Either the abuse will never be discovered, resources will be unavailable, or there will be a lack of awareness of what help is actually available or why outside assistance is important.

One of the major reasons why child abuse of any kind creates the risk of ongoing problems is because it occurs as the child is developing and changing rapidly in response to many environmental demands.

Children are remarkably resilient creatures. While this resilience is one cause for optimism about the eventual outcome of abuse, it also makes it easy for frightened adults to wish away the potential side effects of victimization. "He is too young to remember," "She doesn't really understand what happened to her," etc., are statements which often describe parental hope rather than childhood reality. Traumatic events can interfere with normal developmental processes if the child is not given the chance to express his feelings and concerns. The kinds of emotional interference and reaction will not only differ from child to child, but also according to the age of the child.

The following sections will discuss the potential impact of sexual abuse at different ages. A brief description of the types of treatment available for victims, family members and incest offenders will be included.

Toddlers and preschool age children are generally facing the developmental task of gaining control over basic physical needs and impulses. Beginning with learning to feed themselves, on through the more complex task of learning to express aggression in socially acceptable ways, young children are required to learn self-control.

Incest distorts the basically protective and educative functions of parenthood to instead meet the needs of the parent or parent substitute. Particularly when they begin early in life, both incest and non-familial abuse overwhelm the child with intense sexual feelings. Many of these abused children have difficulty with the basic level of self-control required in a normal day care or nursery setting. They require therapeutic settings where staff are specially trained to respond in a firm but accepting way to incidents of sexual and aggressive behavior that would not be tolerated in everyday settings.

School age children are faced with more complex social demands, from handling authority figures to academic pressures. Disturbances in the parent-child relationship characteristic of incest make it extremely difficult for them to function independently because they lack the solid base of security and acceptance children need.

Incestuous families may also isolate children systematically from peers, either because of the abuser's jealousy or fear of discovery. This isolation prevents normal opportunities for social development. Other forms of extra-familial sexual abuse may leave children initially too frightened, anxious, or angry to focus on anything but their victimization. Their acting out of these feelings may cause a wide range of negative responses from the environment.

Adolescents are dealing with the need to separate from their parents and form their own stable, individual identities. Teens in incestuous families are often responding chaotically to the lack of age and role distinctions they see around them. Mother and daughter may relate as competitive peers or a father may behave like a suspicious boyfriend. The difficulty of growing up and leaving home in a successful manner is greatly exacerbated by this lack of clear boundaries.

In both incest and non-familial abuse, girls of this age may become aware of the possibility of pregnancy resulting from sexual abuse for the first time. Both sexes, but boys in particular, may feel intense guilt because of their increased capacity for sexual response. This can have a strong impact on teens' ability to make sexual feelings a comfortable part of their emerging identity.

WHO IS THE PATIENT?

At times, the emphasis on treatment of the victim may lead us to ignore the other victims of sexual abuse, as well as the perpetrator. Especially when the abuser is a family member, all members of the family have a problem and require assistance. The secrecy, guilt, and denial that occur as part of incest will have serious effects even on non-victimized siblings. Marital difficulties may not be acknowledged but are always present. In situations where abuse occurs outside the family, other family members, including siblings, can generally benefit from the opportunity to discuss their feelings and fantasies about what has happened and what can be expected in the future.

When treatment focuses solely on the child victim, this may have the unintentional effect of reinforcing the child's belief that he or she is the problem. Aside from the pressing need for help for all family members, this is another reason to keep in mind that the child is merely the most visible victim of sexual abuse.

A WORD ABOUT OFFENDER TREATMENT

Because we know that a single offender frequently has more than one victim during a lifetime, the importance of offender treatment as a preventive measure is evident. However, an additional benefit of offender treatment is that it often allows offenders to accept responsibility for the sexual abuse and thereby relieve children of the burden of proving they are telling the truth.

When family members are abusers, special programs called *Incest Offenders Diversion Programs* can allow carefully selected offenders to "divert" from prison to treatment if they meet a variety of criteria. These programs accept primarily first time, non-violent, parent offenders who are willing to participate in up to two years of out-patient treatment. Individual, marital, and family therapy, plus open admission of guilt to other family members, are typically required. Diversion programs recognize the importance of the parent-child relationship and remove the fear of imprisonment as a barrier to change.

FORMS OF THERAPY

Individual, marital, and family therapy have all been mentioned above in the treatment of sexual abuse victims. In most situations, some combination of these approaches is used. With young children, individual therapy usually relies heavily on the use of play as the primary means of communication. With older children, group modes of treatment become increasingly useful. Incest offenders and spouses both can also benefit from group participation.

Although support groups appear to be most useful when coupled in some way with more individualized therapy, groups such as Parents United (Parents Anonymous) can help many incestuous families to feel less alone and less stigmatized. When individual therapy has progressed to the point where the incest offender has been able to accept responsibility for the abuse and the non-abusive spouse has taken steps toward appropriately protecting the child victim, family therapy may focus on a variety of family issues.

The underlying goals of family therapy are to increase generational boundaries, improve communication, and provide a safer home. Therapy for family and victim is important in non-familial abuse to help the victim cope and to help parents and other family members channel their guilt, anger, and fears about the abuse.

THERAPEUTIC GOALS AND ACTIVITIES

This section will focus on some of the goals of therapy with victims' families, with special emphasis on the younger age group. Also included are some therapeutic activities that are often helpful as part of play therapy with young sexual abuse victims. These activities are presented as part of a therapeutic relationship and not as a substitute for professional assistance. A child psychiatrist, psychologist, or social worker, with training and supervision in the area of sexual abuse, is the best choice for treatment. In ideal situations, a multi-disciplinary team will coordinate treatment for the entire family.

The local Child Protective Services Unit, usually connected with the county social services bureau, can often suggest the names of competent professionals. Nationwide, the Family Services Association often provides resources. Local groups of child psychiatrists, psychologists and social workers often give referrals to their membership. Educational materials about sexual abuse and its treatment are available from the National Committee for the Prevention of Child Abuse and Neglect, Suite 1250, 332 S. Michigan Ave., Chicago, IL 60604. Another resource is the National Organization of Parents United, P.O. Box 952, San Jose, CA 95108.

GOALS

While all victims of sexual abuse share certain common difficulties, the developmental level of the child, both at the onset of sexual abuse and at the time of discovery, will be very important in determining the focus of intervention. For example, while difficulty with trust is almost always evident at all age levels, children who have been victimized for years or who have previously reported the abuse to no avail, tend to show far more serious problems with trust than other victims.

Other potential areas for intervention are the child's guilt and interpretation of his own responsibility for the abuse, mixed feelings toward the abuser or other family members, fear of being permanently "different," shame about pleasurable feelings, guilt over the consequences of reporting, fear of rejection and/or repetition of the abuse, and fear of physical damage. Older children may fear homosexuality, vaguely defined notions of frigidity, or becoming sex offenders themselves.

Therapy must help the individual child sort out his own concerns and provide the support and information needed to move on with childhood. Depending on the developmental tasks facing a particular child, therapy will quickly come to include working with that child to function successively closer to age level.

For example, self-control through verbalization of impulses and feelings will become a focus of play therapy with young children. Indirect expression of fear and anxiety typical of pre-schoolers can be interpreted for the child in a reassuring manner. Most of the play techniques suggested below rely heavily on fantasy to allow child and therapist opportunities to handle frightening feelings on a safe level.

Older children will be better able to deal with a more problem-solving orientation where they can begin to identify and more directly express their concerns. However, because ongoing abuse can interfere so directly with normal psychological development, therapists must be aware that they are often dealing with children who are emotionally younger than their chronological age.

Some resources on treatment include a book entitled *Sexual Abuse of Young Children: Evaluation and Treatment* (MacFarlane and Wateran), and the *Handbook of Clinical Intervention in Child Sexual Abuse* (Sgroi).

ACTIVITIES

Puppet Play: Puppets allow the child to actively identify with a character and express feelings at a safer distance. The very young child (under four years old) often does best when a variety of ready-made animal and human puppets are available. Children over age four enjoy making simple puppets of their own design.

Basic paper bags (lunch size works best for small hands), crayons, and markers can produce a variety of characters. The child can be encouraged to identify the puppets in some way and to involve them in play with other kinds of "creatures" as desired.

The therapist tries to strike a balance between encouraging children to talk about some of their feelings through puppets and interfering or structuring the situation too much. In most cases, the actual details of the sexual abuse have been uncovered in interviews with social service personnel, and hopefully have been videotaped, to avoid the need for repetition. Play therapy is then free to focus on the child's *interpretation* of the abusive situation rather than the detailed recounting or repetition of questions and answers.

Doll Play: Traditional play therapy has always used the doll house and family characters in order to allow the child to express relevant themes of family life. Larger scale dolls are also used frequently. Anatomically correct dolls are important in the treatment, as well as the evaluation, of sexual abuse because they concretely demonstrate the therapist's acceptance of sexual topics and provide a medium through which children can communicate their feelings about sexuality.

Mutual Storytelling: Originally popularized by Gardner, this involves asking the child to make up a story "of your very own, with a beginning, middle and end." The child is encouraged to be sure it is "made-up", often a difficult distinction for younger storytellers. The story is taped on audio or videotape and played back to the child.

This is generally a very enjoyable experience that makes the child feel listened to and important. The therapist then tries to identify the underlying feeling, need, or conflict in the story and makes up a story to identify the problem or suggest alternate coping patterns within a fantasy mode. While the themes of their stories are as diverse as the children themselves, sexually abused children often focus on bodily integrity, vulnerability, rage, and fear of rejection.

The Personal Book: Children love to be the center of attention. Nursery school teachers have known for years that "Me Books" can be effective self-esteem builders for children. This kind of project can be incorporated into therapy with pre-school age children who are invited to make a "Feeling Book."

Quick as a Cricket (Wood) can often be used as a very loose model to get children started. The child is then invited to pick a feeling and draw a picture about it. Older children can add a story about that feeling. The completed collection takes many weeks of work and is often a source of pride for the children. In many cases, the child is willing and eager to share this book with parents in family therapy, where it can help as a practice tool in sharing feelings.

In cases where children have had extreme difficulty in discussing the abusive experience with anyone, they are sometimes able to communicate their feelings about what has happened to them through their book. *Something Happened and I'm Scared to Tell* can also serve as a beginning model for this activity.

Empowering: Therapy also must focus on providing the child with the skills and competence to handle potentially abusive situations in the future. Just like adult victims of crime, children often experience a sense of helplessness and vulnerability that can lead to further victimization.

Many of the sex education materials recommended earlier can be used in therapy to help reconstruct children's fantasies about what has happened to them and their bodies as a result of sexual abuse. In addition, some of the excellent preventive books on sexual abuse can be read together, first with the therapist, and then with parents, to give the child both permission and skills to handle another situation.

Sometimes a Cigar is just a Cigar: As Freud said, not everything needs to be interpreted. Much of play therapy with any child focuses on shared activity in a safe, accepting environment and on integrating this into the parent-child relationship. The suggestions listed above are some ways of communicating within this therapeutic relationship.

COMMON BEHAVIOR PROBLEMS

Many of the common signs and symptoms of child sexual abuse discussed in earlier segments remain persistent behavior problems even after the actual abuse has ended. Parents, foster parents, and school personnel often seek advice and suggestions from mental health professionals about the self-defeating patterns of child victims. While it is difficult to generalize about individual behavior patterns, the following suggestions are frequently helpful in responding to the needs of sexually abused youngsters.

Education about precocious sexual behavior: As mentioned previously, this can range from a preoccupation with masturbation to aggressive attempts to force other children into sex play. Interactions with adults can also be highly sexualized. The latter pattern seems most likely to occur between female victims and the significant males in their lives. Foster fathers, male teachers, etc. can be informed about this possibility in advance so that they can emotionally prepare themselves and intellectually plan how to respond in a therapeutic manner.

Foster mothers may find themselves feeling jealous and excluded by a child's attempts to re-create the "special" relationship shared previously with the abuser.

Close supervision: Close adult supervision, particularly during peer play, is initially important so that highly sexualized situations can be quickly and calmly interrupted and redirected. This need for supervision should be an important consideration in foster placements involving any preschoolers because of the likelihood that traumatic experiences will be acted out in play. In my experience, this is a common cause of early placement failures involving young abuse victims.

Coordination with nursery, day care or school personnel: While many people fear that a child may be stigmatized if the sexual abuse becomes known, I find that this risk is greatly outweighed by the need for cooperation between school, family, and therapist. While most day care centers and schools are more than willing to learn more about handling sexually abused children and their difficulties, rigid, anti-sexual attitudes on the part of such institutions can compound the distress of even the youngest victims and their families.

Training and support for foster parents who take in abuse victims: These families take on one of the most difficult jobs in our society, frequently without benefit of training or recognition. At a minimum, support and discussion groups which involve experienced and inexperienced foster parents should be available. Ready access to mental health services is also needed.

Involvement of non-abused siblings in therapy: We need to ensure that siblings also have some knowledge of how to handle sexual advances from others.

Adult acceptance of the child: Acceptance should be coupled with clear, firm limits on the behavior in question. This is particularly important when caregivers are faced with intense, aggressive outbursts. Rejection is especially threatening to children who have been abused in some way. Physical punishment is almost always counter-productive with abused children.

Structure: Structure, in the form of predictable schedules, clear behavioral limits, and behavior modification plans, can also be quite reassuring to children whose internal impulse controls have been disrupted by abuse.

Modelling of appropriate ways of expressing anger: This modelling is best done in a non-threatening environment. Children who have witnessed the behavior of out-of-control adults are often terrified to feel anything. They are especially in need of demonstrations that feelings can be safely expressed.

***Recognize that these behaviors are the child's way
of making some sense out of what has happened***:
With safety, support and structure, almost all abused
children show some significant behavioral gains.

Trust takes time: Difficulty in trusting others is
probably the most common and long lasting effect of
both physical and sexual abuse. Parents and foster
parents need not become discouraged or feel rejected if
they cannot change this behavior pattern quickly. As
one teenage victim of chronic abuse told me, "I like
this (foster) family. I know they want me to tell them
my feelings, but I'm not taking any chances." Adults
must be willing to patiently earn whatever amount of
trust a victimized child is capable of feeling.

Once again, this is merely an overview of some of the
more typical problem behaviors of sexually abused
children. Many other kinds of difficulties that occur,
particularly over long periods, may be more difficult to
clearly relate to the abuse itself.

ANNOTATED READING OF
Something Happened And I'm Scared To Tell

A brief discussion of topics relevant to each page of the book *Something Happened and I'm Scared to Tell* will be offered in this section. Afterwards, some suggestions on establishing a dialogue with the child are presented. These focus on helping the child interpret or discuss the character and what is happening, or move to the next, more intimate step of relating personally to the story.

This will be most helpful if the adult has previously formed a relationship with the child. It is also helpful to intersperse open-ended questions about the child's feelings with personal disclosures or comments to prevent a question and answer format from developing.

Even a child who is not yet ready to share the experience of sexual abuse can benefit from reading this book with a nurturing adult if the relationship is non-threatening and proceeds at the child's pace.

PAGE 1: The character's sex is deliberately vague and can be left up to the reader to determine.

For discussion: Character's expression, what feelings it might indicate, how children handle big worries, child's personal experience with this.

PAGE 2: The lion looks both friendly and threatening, similar to the way a new adult may appear to a child in many situations.

For discussion: How the lion is viewed by the child, what his motives may be.

PAGE 3: These represent examples of threats which are particularly frightening to young children since they are so intensely dependent on their parents.

For discussion: How the reader reacts to the character's fears, how he/she feels about the possibility of parental rejection.

PAGE 4: The idea that some grownups do bad things is paired with a reminder that other grownups will not necessarily side with each other against the child.

For discussion: Happy vs. scary secrets and how the child distinguishes between the two, feelings about "telling."

PAGE 5: The possibility of physical abuse is included because family violence is frequently directly or indirectly involved with sexual abuse. "Being bad" is one of the biggest fears a child faces when confiding in an adult about a new experience. This child models asking directly for adult reassurance, something which a frightened victim would probably be unable to do under the circumstances.

For discussion: Reader's reaction to the character's feelings of "badness" and his/her own self concept.

PAGE 6: Older children are often preoccupied with the concepts of "fairness" and "fault." They cannot make abstract generalizations to guide them in deciding who is responsible for something. The lion tries to focus on adult responsibility for adult behavior.

For discussion: Reader's ideas about the concept of "fault" and "blame."

PAGE 7: The fear of rejection by peers becomes increasingly important as the child develops. In addition, a question like this often masks a child's own negative feelings about himself.

For discussion: How child feels toward the character and what he/she thinks will happen.

PAGE 8: Reassurance from other children is one way to convey that an abusive incident(s) does not change the child's identity. She/he is still the same person and is still cared for and loved.

PAGE 9: Here the child learns that many other children have similar problems and feelings that are also very confusing to them. The willingness of adults to listen, believe, and stop the problems is clearly stated.

For discussion: Reader's reaction to the value of telling the truth, how adults are perceived as responding when he or she shares a problem.

PAGE 10-11: The lion suggests that there are often many alternative people children can trust. The child is not totally isolated. The need for telling and telling "if no one listens" is included as a reminder that this is not always easy.

For discussion: Reader's own difficulties in talking with adults, how a child chooses someone in whom to trust and confide.

PAGE 12: One abusive incident is described in general terms. Details are left vague so there is minimal interference with the child's own experiences. The emphasis is on the child's feelings about the difference between good and bad touches and those characteristics.

For discussion: What feelings the character is showing, how the reader would tell good touches from bad touches.

PAGE 13: Basic words are introduced to give the child the vocabulary to describe his experience and the permission to talk about his body with a grownup.

For discussion: Child's knowledge of these terms, use of other words for genitals.

PAGE 14: Children, like adults in stressful situations, often try to block out painful and frightening memories by not thinking about them. The lion offers an alternative viewpoint.

For discussion: How sad feelings are expressed by reader and/or family, events which have caused sadness.

PAGE 15: The lion reassures the child that talking about painful things and showing sad feelings on the outside is safe and acceptable.

For discussion: Reader's reaction to the character's crying, feelings about crying by himself or herself.

PAGE 16: Some children focus on their anger over abuse while others feel primarily fear or guilt. Whatever the order or pattern of feelings, all three feelings are always present on some level. The issue of ambivalence, having two feelings at the same time, is very disturbing to most children. The lion accepts both feelings uncritically.

For discussion: When angry feelings are acceptable, reader's own experience of mixed feelings.

PAGE 17: The lion identifies the helplessness which is often the basis of a child's anger.

For discussion: How child views helplessness and copes with angry feelings toward powerful figures.

PAGE 18: Words provide a small source of control for a young child. "Naming" provides a concrete way of handling a problem as something identifiable.

For discussion: Does the child already know the term "sexual abuse?" What is his/her definition?

PAGE 19: These examples focus on the motivations and problems of abusers, not victims. They suggest that abusers may sometimes love or care for victims even if their behavior is unacceptable. This in turn makes it just as "okay" for the victim to continue to love an abuser as to be angry with him. Since in incest there is often an ongoing relationship between victim and abuser, it is important to validate both positive *and* negative feelings.

For discussion: How familiar the child is with the concept of sexual abuse? Does he or she know somebody who has been sexually abused? (If so, it can be very important to learn what happened to the victim according to the child's perceptions.)

PAGE 20-21: The issue of physical abuse is re-introduced here in order to interpret some of the reasons for violence. Another reason for including it here is to show that grown ups can have problems showing different feelings. The importance of learning how to show loving and angry feelings is clearly demonstrated.

For discussion: How anger is expressed by the child as well as other family members, how is it acceptable to show anger?

PAGE 22: The child's fear of closeness and difficulty trusting another person is highlighted.

For discussion: Reader's feelings about love and being loved, whom he or she feels loved by, and by whom would they wish to be loved.

PAGE 23: Positive alternatives to sexual and physical abuse demonstrate that there are many good things about showing affection and other feelings to others. A child may find the expression of any intense feelings particularly threatening after abuse.

For discussion: Child's preferences for giving and receiving affection.

PAGE 24: Child and lion are pictured in a playful interaction to illustrate that touch, playfulness, and affection can be fun and safe.

For discussion: Character's expression and the feelings it might represent.

PAGE 25: Since young children lack a clear concept of time, they need frequent reassurance that painful feelings and experiences will not hurt as badly forever. The lion is praising the child's bravery in sharing frightening events. This is one of the most important kinds of reassurance we can offer to the child victim who takes this risk.

For discussion: Reader's feelings towards character and what he or she has done, fantasies about what will happen in the future.

PAGE 26: The child and lion are playing confidently. The child rides the lion happily, suggesting that children can be strong and competent too.

For discussion: How reader might handle this problem in the same situation, what might make it hard to tell, response to the story, opportunity to share scary secrets when the child is ready.

REFERENCES

Books

Ames, L.B. and Ilg. F. *Your Two (Three, Four, etc.) Year Old.* Gesell Institute of Child Development, Dell Publishing Co., New York: 1976-1979.

Briggs, D. Corkille. *Your Child's Self Esteem.* Doubleday & Co., New York: 1970.

Dodson, F. *How to Discipline with Love.* Signet New American Library, New York: 1978.

Elkind, D. *The Hurried Child.* Addison-Wesley Publishing Co., Boston: 1981.

Finkelhor, D. *A Sourcebook on Child Sexual Abuse.* Sage Publications, CA: 1986.

Finkelhor, D. *Child Sexual Abuse: New Theory and Research.* Free Press, New York: 1984.

Freiberg, S. *The Magic Years.* Scribner & Sons, New York: 1959.

Freeman, L. *It's MY Body.* Parenting Press, Inc., Seattle: 1983.

Gardner, R. *Psychotherapeutic Approaches to the Resistant Child.* J. Aronson, Inc., New York: 1975.

Gordon, T. *Parent Effectiveness Training.* P. H. Wyden, New York: 1970.

Hart-Rossi, J. *Protect Your Child from Sexual Abuse.* Parenting Press, Inc., Seattle: 1984.

Kempe, R. & Kempe, C.H. *The Common Secret.* W.H. Freeman & Co., New York: 1984.

MacFarlane, K. & Waterman, J. *Sexual Abuse of Young Children: Evaluation and Treatment.* Guilford Press, New York: 1986.

Mayle, P. *Where Did I Come From?* Lyle Stewart Press, NJ: 1973.

Rogers, F. *Mr. Rogers Talks with Parents.* Berkley Books, New York: 1983.

Sgroi, S. *Handbook of Clinical Intervention in Child Sexual Abuse.* Lexington Books, MA: 1982.

Sheffred, M. *Where Do Babies Come From?* Alfred Knopf Books, New York: 1981.

Wachter, O. *No More Secrets for Me.* Little, Brown & Co., Boston: 1983.

Wood, A. *Quick as a Cricket.* Play Spaces International, Sudbury, MA: 1982.

Records, Videos, Games

"Everyone Makes Mistakes": from *Three Stories*. A Golden Book Video, Sesame Street Co., New York: 1985.

"Mr. Rogers: You Are Special." Record or cassette, Family Communications, Pittsburgh: 1970.

"The Talking, Feeling & Doing Game." Creative Therapeutics, NJ: 1973.

Books Available from Parenting Press by Mail

Something Happened and I'm Scared to Tell: _____
A Book for Young Victims of Abuse, $3.95

Something Is Wrong At My House: A Book for _____
Children About Parents' Fighting, $3.50

It's MY Body: A Book to Teach Young _____
Children to Resist Uncomfortable Touch, $3.50

Protect Your Child from Sexual Abuse: _____
A Parent's Guide, $5.00

Helping Abused Children: A Book for Those _____
Who Work with Sexually Abused Children,
$6.95

Name _____

Address _____

City _____

State _____ Zip _____

Order Subtotal	Shipping
$ 0-$10	add $1.25
$10-$25	add $2.25
$25-$50	add $3.25

Subtotal _____

Shipping _____

*Sales Tax _____

Total _____

Parenting Press, Inc.
7744 31st Ave. N.E., #825
P.O. Box 15163
Seattle, WA 98115

*Washington state residents add 8.1%